CV Exa

-Unique and effective CV examples

-Different types explained and optimised with

 action words and keywords

-Killer attention-grabbing personal statements

Jas Gates

TABLE OF CONTENTS

Introduction

CV Examples can be used as a guide to help you prepare your CV during your job hunt. The book covers a wide range of industries and sectors.

Each example CV begins with a personal statement which you can use to construct your own unique and highly individual statement.

Your CV is your opportunity to sell yourself to potential employers. The key is to identify your key achievements and skill set relevant to the positions applied for. You can use one CV for multiple positions to save time as opposed to having to customise each CV to the different positions.

I strongly recommend going for the role that you really want and are most suitable for rather than settling for second best. A time when you may need more than one CV is if you are applying for completely distinct roles in different sectors.

There are several types of CVs, and this book covers the most common ones. The layouts are not set in stone.

The important thing to remember is to have your personal statement at the top, followed by your strongest skill set, work history then education.

Hobbies and interests do not always have to be included unless you have adequate space for them or some of the interests or hobbies are relevant to your profession.

Key achievements and an additional information section can sometimes help you sell yourself more convincingly to the employer.

School Leaver CV

A school leaver CV needs to focus on the main subjects studied, any skills gained, and any volunteering or paid work placement experience.

Curriculum Vitae

Name: Joe Smith **Tel:** 0700000000 **Email:** name@gmail.com

Personal Statement A school leaver seeking an opportunity to gain and develop sales and marketing experience. Recently helped raise funds for a charity that helps the homeless. Reliable, punctual, looking for a challenge, and eager to learn fast. Definitely not afraid of hard work. Would consider an apprenticeship or internship to kickstart my career.

Skills IT skills, communication, customer service, telephone skills, sales skills, people skills, communication skills

Work Experience
July 2021 - Aug 2021 **Part-Time Temp Volunteer Charity Fundraiser**
A Charity, London
Completed a one-day intensive training program on how to fundraise. Approached members of the public on the street to explain the objectives of the charity and convince them to donate. Enhanced scripts that were used to entice prospective donors. Generated a significant number of leads. Managed to occasionally achieve weekly targets. Boosted morale amongst team workers. Gained invaluable experience and developed several skills that are potentially transferable.

Education
A-levels: English, Computing, Mathematics
London Sixth Form College, London (Sept 2021 - June 2022)

8 GCSEs: Chemistry, Biology, Physics, Computer Science, English Language, French, Spanish
High School, London (Sept 2019 - June 2021)

Languages: Basic French and Spanish

Awards: Chess player of the month (Feb 2017)
Inspirational student of the year winner (2018)

Extracurricular Activities: Cycling, Athletics, Fencing, Climbing, Chess, Squash, Golf

Additional Information: Helping the homeless in my spare time.

Internship CV

With little or no job experience, your CV needs to focus on your skills, education, and interests. This example can also be used for seeking an apprenticeship.

Curriculum Vitae

Mary Jays

Address: Luton Tel: 0700000000 Email: name@ymail.com

Personal Statement I am a passionate university art student and have recently completed artwork focusing on fine art and digital art. I am determined to utilise my artistic skills and relevant knowledge towards making a commendable start to a career in the art world. Completing an internship program would allow me to contribute to the organisation by assisting in the running of the art exhibitions and gallery.

Skills: Communication skills, numerical skills, information technology, problem-solving skills, team working skills, photographic skills, drawing, organisational skills, creative skills, digital marketing skills

Education
Sep 2016 - June 2019 **BA Fine Art** Open University
The course focused on the incorporation of fine arts into digital media (final year dissertation). Relevant modules: Critical and Contextual Studies, Visual Intelligence, Drawing, photography.

Work Experience
Dec 2021 - Feb 2022 **Part-time Volunteer** Art Museum, Luton
Key Responsibilities: Meeting and greeting visitors of the museum, revamping the museum's art collections, categorising collections, and assisting other departments whenever required.

Achievements: Exhibited some of my artwork in a local social club. Created some book illustrations and a book cover for an author on a voluntary basis to expand on my experience. Created an Instagram account where I showcased my artwork online.

Additional Information: I would be willing to work on a trial basis for the first week to confirm whether I have the appropriate skills required. I want to also prove to you that I could fit in and work well with the other work colleagues because I believe that good teamwork is a key component to the success of any art gallery business.

Student Work Placement CV

A student work placement CV needs to focus on the skills, main university course modules studied, and final year project ideas.

Curriculum Vitae

Craig Charles

Address: Romford **Tel:** 0770000000 **Email:** name@yahoo.com

Personal Statement A second-year Business Studies student at the University of London, on track, to receive a 2:2. Attended a business start-up show, to understand more about various businesses across different industry sectors. I am now looking for a one-year placement where I can apply my business acumen, skills, and knowledge.

SKILLS: Presentation skills, Problem-solving, Microsoft Office

Work Experience
Sept 2020 - to date **Part-Time Retail Volunteer,** Romford
Local Charity Shop
Stock replenishment, sorting and pricing stock, window dressing, advising customers, surpassed monthly sales goals

May 2016 - July 2018 **Retail Assistant,** London
London Retail Outlet
Provided excellent customer service in a fast-paced retail environment. Achieved personal sales targets in line with KPI objectives. Other duties included answering telephone inquiries, stocktaking, and operating till.

Education
Sept 2019 - Present **BA Business Studies** University of London
Main Course Modules: human resource management, finance and accounting, marketing, operations management, information systems
Final year project idea: Why some business start-ups fail

2016 - 2018 **A-Levels:** Maths (A), Business (B), Chemistry (B)

2011 - 2016 **9 GCSEs**: Maths, English, French, Art, Geography, History, Science, Humanities, Sociology

Additional Information: My ultimate career goal will be dictated by the work placement experience gained and further research. I look forward to the challenge of creating an impact in the commercial world.

References are available from my course director and previous employer.

Entry Level CV

An entry-level CV is used to apply for entry-level work; jobs that require little or no previous work experience.

Curriculum Vitae

Jay Mann

Address: Croydon Mobile: 0770000000 Email:name@email.com
LinkedIn: linkedin.com/in/_ _ _

Personal Statement A future graphic designer seeking a junior graphic designer position in London. I am determined to utilise my creative digital design skills and unlock my full potential whilst breaking into the world of digital media. The online design portfolio of my personal design work is accessible via my personal website and LinkedIn profile.

Skills: Internet skills, good business acumen, team motivator, analytical thinker, proactive problem solver, creative design skills, web design

Experience
2018 - 2020 **Fashion Retail Sales Assistant** Fashion Store, Croydon
Helping customers find their style, introducing colour palette per season, offering a gift-wrapping service, pricing and displaying items, stock-taking, promotions, customer complaint queries, returns, and refunds

Education
Graphic Design (BTEC HND) 2014 - 2016
London College of Applied Arts, London
Main Course Modules: Printmaking, Branding & Identity, Art Direction

Software Packages: Adobe products i.e., Photoshop, Illustrator, CorelDraw, SketchUp 3D Modelling Software, Microsoft Office i.e., Excel, PowerPoint, Word, Outlook, Access

Languages: English, Latvian, German (Basic)

Interests/Hobbies Sketching/drawing, museums, photography, writing, music, web design, digital art, painting, computer games, singing

Additional Information: Designed a poster on a voluntary basis to help promote an event in the local community.

Chronological CV

A chronological CV displays the contents (work history and education) in descending chronological order.

Curriculum Vitae

Lisa Mills

Address: Greater London

Email: name@hotmail.com Tel: 0700000000

Personal Statement

Responsible English-speaking Secretary/Assistant Researcher with over 5 years of experience working for a Japanese company. Extensive experience providing secretarial support for the directors, deputy directors, and researchers who were either seconded from Japan or were Japanese living in the UK. My greatest strengths are loyalty, dedication, accuracy, and having the ability to adapt to new working environments and concepts.

Skills

Microsoft Excel (intermediate level), Microsoft Word (advanced level), communication skills, writing skills, admin skills, telephone skills, secretarial skills, proofreading & editing skills

Work Experience

2014 - 2021 **Secretary/Assistant Researcher**

A Foundation for Communications, London

Obtaining and summarising information for research purposes.

Liaising with the payroll provider and bank on matters regarding change of directors (their arrival to & departure from the UK).

Informing payroll providers of salary details and any changes in information.

Assisting when required with the creation of questionnaires & follow-up of inquiries.

Attending webinars and summarising discussions for the director.

Included in the panel for the job interviewing process to recruit new staff.

Assisting in training new staff.

Successfully managed relocation of London office and remained within the allocated budget.

2012 - 2013 **Freelance Content Writer** (Home-based)

Proofreading and editing of clients' website content including some content writing. Clients included London Course Finder, the Job Aid Charity, and an eBook by a self-published author listed on the Amazon website. Also helped international students with proofreading and editing their assignments and final year dissertations.

2005 - 2011 **Customer Care Administrator**

The Club, London

Answering the telephone and responding to all customer inquiries including dealing with customer complaints.

Assisting the communication and customer service teams, process, and post documentation. Help maintain the filing system.

Education

Higher Education College 2001 - 2004 London

BA Japanese Studies, Japanese Language & Art. This included 6 months of study at Tokyo University, Japan to which I received a certificate showing successful completion of training courses in Japanese.

Southgate Sixth Form 1999 - 2001

North London

2 A Levels English Literature, Art & Design

Hobbies & Interests

Horse riding, painting, drawing, writing poetry and short stories, reading, movies, gym, martial arts

Skills-Based CV

A skills-based CV needs to focus on the skills (including transferable skills) and be used when your relevant work experience for the post is limited.

Curriculum Vitae

David Smith

Address: Slough Tel: 0700000000 Email: name@outlook.com

PERSONAL STATEMENT

A recent graduate with some intensive work and voluntary experience. I have skills and attributes to offer the business world including leadership, analytical thinking, problem-solving, team working, communication, and social media. I am keen to join a graduate program and make a positive impact from day one.

SKILLS: teamwork, organisational, negotiation, communication, leadership, social media, computing

Education

2016 - 2019 A University, London

BA(Hons) Marketing 2:2

2009 - 2016 Slough School, Slough

A-levels: English, Mathematics. AS level Sociology

8 GCSEs: maths, science, chemistry, art, biology, physics, computing, history

Employment

2020 - 2021 **Office Assistant** A Travel Centre, London

Typical office duties i.e., answering the telephone, filing, word processing, photocopying, scanning, emailing, etc.
Email marketing and website content management.
Making business travel arrangements for senior management.

2019 - 2020 **Stockroom Assistant** The Warehouse Centre, West London

Performed stockroom assistant duties in a warehouse setting. Taking stock of incoming materials and supplies as per invoice. Packing products.

SKILLS

Teamwork Skills

Worked well with the office manager, secretary, and other staff members to help ensure that the company's goals were met.

Organisational Skills

Organised events i.e., the office Christmas party and product launch events.

Negotiation Skills

Negotiated the price of the coach tickets for a school trip. Also negotiated the guesthouse rates where the students were staying.

Written communication

For my university course, I had written essays, reports and seminar papers under strict guidelines. Created content for a blog.

Verbal communication

Dealing with customer complaints as well as communicating with suppliers. Creating and giving presentations to large and small groups at the university.

Leadership Skills

Responsible for training new staff on company policies and procedures.

IT Skills

Competent user of software applications. Knowledge of bespoke software packages.

Social media marketing skills

Designed a Facebook business page and LinkedIn business page to help promote the company's brand.

Presentation Skills

Presented a PowerPoint presentation for my final year university project.

Combined CV

A combined CV merges a skills-based CV with a chronological one.

Curriculum Vitae

Mandy Bee

Address: Guildford Tel:070000000 Email: name@email.com

LinkedIn: linkedin/in/_ _ _

Personal Statement

Energetic, self-motivated, and creative, I am seeking a position in business management. My business admin skills and office management skills can be applied within any industry sector. I have intensive office experience and am adaptable to new challenges. Available for a one-week trial and always striving to contribute towards business development.

Education

2014 -2017 **BA(Hons) Business Studies**

University of Surrey

Guildford

2011 – 2014 A Sixth Form College

A-Levels: English, Science

Guildford

Work Experience

2019 - To Date **Business Administrator**

Estates Agency, London

Advised sales staff on how to enhance their sales strategies.

Arranged meetings with shareholders.

Ensured that the staff were working to the required standard.

Forecasted sales for the next two years.

Identified problems with company hardware and software.

Resolved issues amongst staff.

2018 - 2019 **Office Manager**

London Plumbers

Augmented work procedures to improve cost-effectiveness.

Integrated new software to interface with the customer relationship management system.

Optimised social media accounts to promote business services.

2017 - 2018 **Office Assistant (Temp)**

ABC Solutions

Secretarial and admin duties i.e., scanning, photocopying, transcribing, emailing, letter writing, document management. Provided first line support via telephone to users.

SKILLS

Leadership – delegated work amongst staff

Teamwork – gave feedback on sales team presentations

Admin – research, typing, document management, order processing

Customer Service – provided after-sales support

Social media – created and added content to social media pages

Telemarketing – cold calling for lead generation

Computing – proficient with Microsoft Windows software

Communication – presented PowerPoint slides on behalf of sales staff

Management skills – managed office staff

Website design skills - created a webpage using WordPress

Sales skills – wrote up and submitted quotations to clients

Languages

Basic French, Intermediate German

Career Break CV

A career break CV is used when the candidate has had time off from working i.e., taking a year off, a long vacation, dealing with health issues, looking after a family member, etc.

Curriculum Vitae

Sandy Evans

Address: Harrow

Email: name@mail.com

Tel: 0770000000

Personal Statement

I am a confident and capable office manager with intensive experience managing a team of in-house consultants and other staff members in the office. A period of absence from the workforce has energised and motivated me to restart my career. For the past two months, having taken on volunteering to refresh my skills, I'm now highly motivated to develop my office management experience and impress my next employer.

Skills:

Capable of all common office management tasks.

Highly organised, conscientious, and professional.

Attentive, caring, and eager to help those in need.

Employment History

Jan 2022 - to date **Office Manager** A Foundation, Wembley

(A charity providing personal support to cancer patients).

Managing databases, ordering stock. Allocated work to staff

Processing donations and other payments. Reporting to senior management.

Key Achievements

Negotiated a new contract with a supplier which cut costs. Ensured the speedy processing of all donations

June 2020 - Dec 2021 Career break

In mid-2020 I took a career break in order to provide round-the-clock care to a family member recovering from a medical illness during the pandemic.

Aiding with household tasks.

Providing transport to and from medical appointments.

Shopping online and organising food deliveries.

March 2018 - May 2020 **Admin Manager** London Business House (Small company providing B2B business consultancy in the Greater London area).

Managing consultants' expenses and timesheets. Manage compliance and stock levels. Engage team members in business activities.

Customer service management

Education And Qualifications

2015 - 2017 **A Levels:** Business Administration, Italian, History

Harrow Sixth Form College

2013 - 2015 **GCSEs:** 10, including Maths and English

Professional Development

Online Cost Management course (2016)

AAT Bookkeeping Foundation (2015)

Additional Skills & Proficiencies

Microsoft word, excel, PowerPoint, outlook, teams collaborating software, conducting zoom meetings

Social Media skills,

Cyber security basics

Languages: English and German

Interests and Hobbies

Cooking, current affairs, social media. reading novels, ice skating, horse riding, salsa

Career Change CV

A career change CV is used when taking on a role that differs from your recent work experience.

Curriculum Vitae

David Parker

Tel: 0770000000 Email: name@outlook.com

Address: Bexley

LinkedIn: linkedin.com/in/_ _ _

Personal Statement

An accountant with five years of experience preparing accounts for several clients changing to a career in counselling because I am passionate about helping people. There are countless people in need of counselling and I have developed strong transferable skills that can be applied to this type of role. I am confident my communication skills and interpersonal skills will enable me to help any employer achieve its objectives. Highly motivated under pressure and empathetic.

Skills

Payroll, sales order processing, purchase order processing, bookkeeping, public speaking, analytical skills, mediation skills

Experience

2015 - 2019 **Accountant** S & Associates, London

Prepared end-of-year accounts in a busy accounting firm.

Uses excel macros to create and manage financial reporting.

2012 - 2015 **Accounts Assistant** A Marketing Ltd, Gravesend

Worked with the chartered accountant on projects for a fast-paced business.

Typed up accounts and managed the client database system including email marketing tasks.

Developed Excel spreadsheet macros.

Maintained company website via the website content management system. Content-writing for optimising websites for search engine marketing.

Education

2013 - 2014 **AAT Level 4**

Online Learning

2012 - 2013 **AAT Level 2 & 3**

Online Learning

2008 - 2012 **BA(Hons) in Accounting & Finance**, Kent University

Excelled in accounts software coursework.

Worked as a computer science teacher's assistant for three semesters.

Additional Information

Participated in the London Marathon, 2018.

Volunteer web admin support for a local homeless non-profit organisation that provides shelter.

Lead weekly yoga classes for fun and self-care.

Worked part-time on an ad-hoc basis for the Samaritans.

Tech Skills

Coding, Debugging, Microsoft Office, Website CMS, Excel (Advanced),

WordPress, Joomla, Magenta, Sage, Sap Modules

Soft Skills

Leadership, teamwork, problem-solving, critical thinking, creativity, public speaking skills, telephone skills, analytical skills

Languages

Basic Italian and French

Personal Interests

Socialising, listening to current affairs, offering help to charities whenever I can, public speaking (member of a local speakers' club)

Technical CV

A technical CV lists the technical skills and work history, which outlines an individual's ability to succeed in a technical role.

Curriculum Vitae

Beverley Lee

Address: London

Email: name@gmail.com Tel: 07777000000

LinkedIn: linkedin/in/_ _ _

Personal Statement

A computer studies graduate with several years of commercial experience in technical roles. I'm seeking a position in app development where I can utilise my coding and design skills. My goal is to join one of the best app development teams in the city to eventually become one of the best and contribute to the successful completion of current and future projects. Willing to work on a one-week trial basis so that I can prove my technical skills and knowledge in the app development sector.

Skills: software development, computer hardware, software testing, sales skills, customer service skills

Education

University of London (2007 - 2011)

BSc (Hons) Computer Studies

Main Modules: java programming, active server pages, object-oriented design methodology, computer systems management, full-stack development

London Sixth Form College (2005 - 2007)

A-levels: computing, maths, physics

10 GCSEs: English language, mathematics, art, biology, chemistry, physics, English literature, law, commerce, geography

Employment

(2015 - to present) **Business Development Manager**

Information Systems Tech, London

Created PowerPoint presentation of IT services.

Presented to a wide range of clients.

Analysed prospective clients' IT requirements.

Prepared sales proposals for the clients.

Demonstrated prototypes of proposed software systems.

Tested new software across different devices and platforms.

2012-2014 **Software Developer**, London Call Centre

Created a CRM system for staff to use to maintain records of prospective and current client data.

Developed an in-house accounts system to automate some of the basic but essential accounting tasks.

Coded macros to manipulate a PowerPoint presentation which was used by the IT consultants to present company services to potential customers.

Volunteering

Helping the homeless in London by cooking and delivering food to key locations across London where homeless living was abundant.

Helped a charity that helped refugees by offering remote complimentary lessons in computing and the internet.

Created a database for a charity to help them streamline and manage applicant data for housing applications.

Technical Skills

Artificial intelligence, Python coding, Blockchain, Internet of Things, databases, app design, and development

Activities and achievements

Member of London University Cricket Team

Runner up in a local cooking competition

References: Two excellent work references and one character reference available on request

Mid-Level CV

A mid-level CV showcases the skills and past relevant work experience in your profession. It should clearly express your precise responsibilities and achievements.

Curriculum Vitae

Donna Tee

Address: London

Email: name@yahoo.co.uk

Tel: 0770000000

Website: www._ _ _

LinkedIn: linkedin.com/in/_ _ _

Instagram: Instagram.com/_ _ _

Twitter: twitter.com/ _ _ _

Personal Statement

A self-motivated all-around senior interior designer with 7+ years of commercial experience. Talented, highly creative and a team player. Eager to join a company to motivate and lead design teams and manage projects from inception to completion. In previous roles completed large-scale projects, managed multiple teams, and grew relationships with vendors and clients.

Skills

Presentation, customer service, negotiation, communication, creative skills, problem-solving, graphic design

Work History

September 2015 - Present **Interior Designer**

A Architects, London

Negotiated deals with new customers.

Created digital prototypes to present to prospective clients.

Managed several commercial projects in the hospitality industry.

Collaborated with suppliers of fabrics and furniture.

Supervised and led the teams on projects.

Trained and influenced the other designers.

2011 - 2013 **Junior Interior Designer**

Jay & Jay, Kingston

Prepared supplies and resources for prospective client meetings.

Researched information gathering relative to programming analysis, space plans, and area calculations.

Published contractual documentation, including plans, and details.

Selected colours and materials as per client requirements.

Drew up illustrations for conceptual prototype designs.

Technical Skills

Adobe products (Photoshop, InDesign, Illustrator), HTML, CSS, AutoCAD, Project management tools, Microsoft PowerPoint, Microsoft Excel, Social media management, Shotcut video editing software

Education

BA(Hons) in Interior Design & Styling

University of London 2008 - 2011

Main course modules: Design, materials and construction, colour in design

2005- 2006 **A levels**

English, Art, maths

London Design School

Languages

Spanish and English

Executive Level CV

An executive-level CV summarises the experience, skills, achievements, and knowledge gained from an established lengthy career.

Curriculum Vitae

Peter Lang

Address: London

Telephone: 070000000

Email: aname@amail.com

Personal Statement

A business professional who has created and developed successful businesses from start-up. Substantial sales & online marketing experience with a proven track record willing to showcase my advanced skills to create the fast results needed to help your business exceed targets and subsequently increase annual turnover.

Skills:

Hard Skills: New business development, managing sales campaigns, developed business strategies, business partner development

Soft Skills: Interpersonal skills, leadership, communication, active learning

Employment History

2015 - 2021 **Managing Director**

London School of Computing,

Created and implemented a marketing plan for maximising business development.

Developed and implemented an in-house student management system.

Implemented company policies and recruitment procedures.

Hosted company events.

2013 - 2015 **Online Marketing Professional**

Tech Co, London

Optimised company website to increase ranking in google and other search engines.

Conducted an email marketing campaign to increase brand awareness.

Created content for the business's social media pages including Facebook, and LinkedIn.

Recruited and trained new sales and marketing staff.

Created and optimised company services brochure.

Converted online brochure to a PowerPoint presentation and subsequently to video format for upload to YouTube.

Education

MBA, London Institute 2011 - 2012

Dissertation on internet marketing

BA Marketing, London Institute 2007 - 2010

Main course modules: digital marketing, social media marketing, business accounting, computer systems management

Certifications

Certified Google Ads Specialist 2013

Certified Amazon Reseller 2014

Additional Activities

Published content about online business start-ups on LinkedIn with over 100k followers and content going viral with up to one million views.

Conferences

2016 - Education Consultancy

2018 - Facebook Ads

Key Achievements

Achieved an annual turnover of over one million from the internet marketing strategies I devised. Reduced advertising expenditure by 30%.

Improved student intake by 25% mainly from google ads campaigns and social media marketing campaigns

Conclusion

Having considered all the examples, you should now have the ability to write a winning CV.

The CV must be attention-grabbing in order for the reader, your prospective employer, to want to take action. The more attention-grabbing the CV, the greater the likelihood of a positive response. The key is to sell yourself persuasively.

List your skills, and responsibilities from earlier positions using action words to add impact and make sure keywords are included that can be picked up from automated tracking systems.

Prior to any interview, whether it is by phone, online, or in-person, remember to refresh your memory with the content of your CV (and cover letter). It is also a clever idea to read through your CV and the job description if you have access to it, to help improve conversation flow when the interview is conducted.

Other CVs which I have not covered in this book are the academic CV and creative CV. An academic CV includes your education, professional appointments, teaching, research, publications, and any awards. The creative CV used by designers enables you, the designer, to display your design skills. There are sufficient examples online that may help inspire you to create your own design. Although the layout depends on your design theme, the content is the same as the traditional CV examples in this book.

The video CV or LinkedIn profile may well replace the CV as we know it and recruiters are always on the lookout for innovative technology such as Blockchain to help prevent CV fraud. But for now, a well-written CV is your foot in the door of your next employer.

Printed in Great Britain
by Amazon

36377613R00015